DIVINE

First published in 2026 by OH
An Imprint of HEADLINE PUBLISHING GROUP LIMITED

1

Disclaimer:
This book has not been licensed, approved, sponsored, or endorsed by Rosalía.

Cataloguing in Publication Data is available from the British Library

ISBN 978-1-03543-661-3

Compiled and written by Malcolm Croft
Editorial: Beth Bishop and Phoebe Hills
Designed and typeset in Avenir by Stephen Cary
Project manager: Russell Porter
Illustration by Ryan Adey
Production: Arlene Lestrade
Printed and bound in China

MIX
Paper | Supporting responsible forestry
FSC® C104740
www.fsc.org

Headline's policy is to use papers that are natural, renewable and recyclable products and made from wood grown in well-managed forests and other controlled sources. The logging and manufacturing processes are expected to conform to the environmental regulations of the country of origin.

HEADLINE PUBLISHING GROUP LIMITED
An Hachette UK Company
Carmelite House, 50 Victoria Embankment, London EC4Y 0DZ

The authorised representative in the EEA is Hachette Ireland, 8 Castlecourt Centre, Dublin 15, D15 XTP3, Ireland (email: info@hbgi.ie)

www.headline.co.uk www.hachette.co.uk

DIVINE

THE LITTLE GUIDE TO ROSALÍA

UNOFFICIAL AND UNAUTHORIZED

CONTENTS

INTRODUCTION – 6

8
CHAPTER
ONE
LA ROSALÍA

38
CHAPTER
TWO
KNOW YOURSELF

68
CHAPTER
THREE
LIKE A PRAYER

98

CHAPTER
FOUR

HURTS LIKE HEAVEN

128

CHAPTER
FIVE

BACK TO THE FUTURE

158

CHAPTER
SIX

SEE THE LIGHT

INTRODUCTION

Rosalía is on a mission from God. Since her arrival on the global stage in 2018, this rebellious, experimental, genre-blending artist has injected electronica into flamenco, and sex (and motorbikes) into spirituality – she's a musical force not to be messed with.

This compact companion sets out to answer the question Rosalía asks in the opening lines of "Saoko" on her 2022 masterpiece MOTOMAMI: "¿Chica, qué dices?" ("Girl, what you sayin'?"). This tiny tome has the answer, in Rosalía's very own words.

Rosalía is the latest – and possibly most revolutionary – solo-name in pop (alongside her idols Beyoncé, Madonna and Adele). And as a classically trained singer, flamenco artist, multi-instrumentalist, brand CEO, nail art pioneer, producer and progressive feminist, she can do it all. Hailed as the "Rihanna of flamenco", she's already one of Spain's greatest musical exports of all time.

She's redefined global pop; fusing tradition with modernity and experimenting boldly with genres –

you never know what Rosalía's going to do next. Her collaborators encompass many of the greats, with stars ranging from Bjork and Pharrell Williams to Bad Bunny and The Weeknd all lining up to work with this special artist.

Armed with a collection of Grammy, BRIT and Billboard awards, Rosalía's talent is beyond question. Her shows are performance *art*: dramatic, high-concept spectacles that have to be seen to be believed. She refuses to conform or be confined – by genre, people's expectations, or even language! – and her free and fluid sound is constantly evolving.

This little guide traces her rise from her Spanish upbringing to her era-defining 2025 album LUX, and is a celebration of everything that makes her one-of-a-kind. If you're new to Rosalía, welcome – you won't be disappointed. And if you're a long-time motobaby – the hilarious collective noun for her loyal fans – then come on in, your girl's about to shine.

CHAPTER ONE

LA ROSALÍA

Welcome to Rosalía's bold, rule-breaking world – Spain's modern-day spiritual superstar.

She came from humble beginnings and grew into one of the most unique voices of her generation. This is her story, told in her own words.

First up: where it all began – her early rise, her faith, her family, and that deep love of flamenco.

25 September 1992

Rosalía Vila Tobella's date of birth in Sant Esteve Sesrovires, a town 20 miles north of Barcelona, in the autonomous community of Catalonia.

The No.1 song in Spain on this day was Snap!'s worldwide hit "Rhythm Is a Dancer".

“

Rhythm is something very primal. You do not choose when you move, you can’t think or premeditate how you’re going to gesticulate. On stage you always have to connect, you have to think of yourself as a channel – and then let your body move on its own.

”

Rosalía, on her love of *saoko* (rhythm) and flamenco moves such as *zapateado* (stamping), *palmas* (clapping) and *braceo* (arm movements) – essential to her identity as a performer, interview with Shaina Joy Machlus, *Tom Tom Magazine*, 22 June 2017

"

Six years ago I think I started to pray more and more and more. *Something* was asking me to do it. Today it is a common practice in my day-to-day life. My faith is something very much alive – because it goes hand in hand with doubt.

"

Rosalía, on her faith, interview with Dídac Piferrer, Marca, 19 March 2026

“

My family didn’t listen to flamenco. In my house, it was The Beatles, Queen, Bob Dylan, a lot of English-language music. I really didn´t have any flamenco input. The closest was with my grandmother. Some weekends when I was with her, she’d be humming Sara Montiel songs, some *copla*. That was the closest, but it wasn’t flamenco.

”

Rosalía, on her beloved grandma, and hearing traditional Spanish poetic and musical forms in her childhood, interview with Judy Cantor-Navas, *Billboard*, 29 October 2018

"

There are a lot of people from Andalusia in my neighborhood. I grew up with children of Andalusian immigrants. The area I grew up in, El Baix Llobregat – it's kind of like Los Angeles and Mexicans. The culture is there, you can breathe it in all around you.

"

Rosalía, on her upbringing in the UNESCO-recognized birthplace of flamenco, Andalusia, interview with Judy Cantor-Navas, *Billboard*, 29 October 2018

"

I don't force things. I can have a wish, and then I let God lead me on the path, bringing me what I need – and always trying to be alert to receive it.

"

Rosalía, on believing in her divine destiny, interview with Marcela Valdes, *The New York Times*, 8 October 2019

“I’m certain that I will be an artist!”

Rosalía, as a 15-year-old contestant on the 2007 Barcelona talent show *Tú Sí Que Vales* (*You’re Worth It*), Spain’s answer to *American Idol*.

Armed with nothing but a guitar, she delivered a stripped-back flamenco performance. The judges weren’t convinced, saying her voice “lacked character” – so she switched it up mid-audition, launching into Alicia Keys’ “No One”! It wasn’t enough. “I think you have a lot of potential,” one judge told her, “but you still don’t know how to bring it out.” That decision hasn’t aged well.

“

Through going on *Tú Sí Que Vales*, I learned that becoming a musician was going to be something that required humility and patience. If I hadn't gone on that show, I probably would have never realized how much I had to work.

”

Rosalía, on being a contestant on Barcelona's reality TV show *Tú Sí Que Vales*, interview with Shaad D'Souza, *The Guardian*, 8 December 2022

“

Nobody in my family was connected to the music industry, so I didn’t know how to *romper el melón* [“break the melon”]* – I don’t know how to say that in English!

”

Rosalía, on breaking through as an artist, interview with Shaad D’Souza, *The Guardian*, 8 December 2022

*In Spain, *romper el melón* is the kind of phrase you use when you’re cracking something open for the first time.

“

I started studying music at 13. I had been telling my parents since I was 10 that I wanted to, but I didn’t start until then. I started with modern music, I studied guitar, piano, I got a taste of *everything*.

”

Rosalía, on her earliest desires to not just play and perform music – but *study* it too, *Billboard*, 29 October 2018

“

I didn’t know anything.
And he taught me everything,
everything, *everything*.

”

Rosalía, on her highly influential flamenco teacher José Miguel Vizcaya ("El Chiqui"), who saw raw talent and masses of potential, interview with Marcela Valdes, *The New York Times*, 8 October 2019

At age seven Rosalía discovered she could sing by belting TV show themes around her family home. She later studied flamenco for six years at the Taller de Músics in Barcelona and trained under renowned virtuoso José Miguel Vizcaya ("El Chiqui", or "Maestro" to Rosalía).

She attended the Catalonia College of Music, graduating in 2017. While studying, she sang in a "thousand" *tablaos* (traditional flamenco venues) and bars across Barcelona, often without pay. "I would ask them to let me sing. Sometimes, they'd pay me with dinner.", she told *The FADER* in 2019.

"

I feel a deep commitment; my mission in life is to make music. I dedicate most of my time and energy to it. Ever since I was little, I knew that's what I wanted to do. I do think that in some way, the love I have for music is similar to the love I feel for God. They're very close to each other for me.

"

Rosalía, on music as her life's mission, interview with Marcos Hassan, Remezcla, 7 November 2025

"

No one in my family plays music. But since I was very little, I would go around the house singing and dancing. And when I was eight, my parents asked me to get up and sing something at a family meal. I had my eyes closed, singing… and when I opened them, the whole family was crying. Everyone. *I swear.* At the time, I didn't understand it. But later, with the passage of time, I thought, 'I have the power to communicate something, and I'd like to develop that.' This is what I want to do with my life.

"

Rosalía, on discovering her musical talent, interview with Philip Sherburne, Pitchfork, 18 September 2018

“

I studied Flamenco at the Taller de Músics here in Barcelona. And got my degree at the ESMUC [Catalonia College of Music]. The idea of studying flamenco is pretty recent, the only places where you can do that are in Barcelona and Córdoba. And in Barcelona, they only accept one person a year, only one person can study for that degree. That was *me!*

”

Rosalía, on being the the sole student selected for the prestigious Catalonia College of Music flamenco degree, interview with Judy Cantor-Navas, *Billboard*, 29 October 2018

“

The world I grew up in is so instantaneous. In flamenco, it's the opposite. Patience. You don't know anything. Start again. Again. It doesn't come out. Again. *Patience*. Four years and I still don't know how to sing. Five years… still not there! And I have to keep going. And it blows my mind, because in flamenco, age is good. The best singers are old. That's what made me think, 'Okay, I have my whole life to get better at this, and I will always have something to learn.'

”

Rosalía, on mastering flamenco – an art that takes a lifetime, interview with Philip Sherburne, Pitchfork, 18 September 2018

“

I really like *San Mateo* [the Gospel of Matthew]. Everything he says, I think it’s bars.

”

Rosalía, on reading the Bible as much as she can, likening scripture to rap lyrics, interview with Laura Snapes, *The Guardian*, 7 November 2025

"

It was like getting pierced by an arrow – it was the purest thing I had ever heard. Camarón de la Isla [an iconic flamenco artist]. He had a voice like an animal. It was like casting a spell. For me, it was as though it wasn't possible to sing more honestly, or viscerally, than him.

"

Rosalía, on first hearing flamenco legend Camarón de la Isla who passed away the same year she was born, interview with Philip Sherburne, Pitchfork, 18 September 2018

"Music has nothing to do with your blood – and it's not territorial. Flamenco doesn't belong to *gitanos* [Romani people]. It doesn't belong to anyone, in fact. And there's nothing wrong with experimenting with it."

Rosalía, on the backlash over accusations of appropriating Romani culture, interview with Ecleen Luzmila Caraballo, Jezebel, 2 November 2018

"For me, there are ideas in different religions that I resonate with. I resonate with Buddhism, Islam, Christianity, Hinduism. I think they all have things I connect with. They resonate with me. I think each religion gives you different things, and I'm equally interested in all of them."

Rosalía, on her celebration of all world faiths,
El País, 9 November 2025

"Justin Timberlake* was everywhere growing up. Destiny's Child was something I'd hear all the time in Spain, too; same with the Spice Girls and Britney Spears. These were icons. They influenced me and I have no problem giving them credit for that. The Spice Girls used to have a tour bus… and I dreamed of having a bus like that!"

Rosalía, on her '90s and '00s musical influences, interview with Michael Cragg, *The Guardian*, 28 June 2019

* Rosalía's "BAGDAD (Cap.7: Liturgia)", from her 2018 album *El Mal Querer*, weaves in a clear, credited interpolation of Timberlake's 2002 hit "Cry Me a River". It's not something Timberlake hands out lightly – he's famously selective with samples – so getting his approval meant something.

“

I love things that are really structured or really loose. I'm not really about finding a middle ground. I like extremes.

”

Rosalía, on her love of pushing things to the limit, interview with Julyssa Lopez, *Vogue*, 15 December 2020

“

Sant Esteve Sesrovires is a landscape of two extremes. It’s a village where there’s a lot of nature. A lot of forest. Beautiful. But also a lot of *fábricas* – factories. Industrial area all around it. A lot of trucks. I remember, since I was a kid, always running around in the forest.

”

Rosalía, on her hometown, a picturesque location also home to lollipop maker Chupa Chups and car manufacturer SEAT, interview with Abby Aguirre, *Vogue*, 10 February 2026

“

I was 15 when I entered a recording studio for the first time. I was so shocked by the fact that there were only men in that session that, since that moment, I've been fighting to have the same number of men and women in the studio.

”

Rosalía, on wanting to reshape the industry and push for real gender equality, interview with Redacción RPP, 14 December 2019

“

My sister Pilar and I work together a lot. I’m very lucky that I get to just keep playing around and having fun like how we used to when we were kids. Her and I love recommending things to each other, we send books to each other. Having a project together is something I feel so grateful about, the fact that my family is involved – my mother, my sister, they’re very important people in my life, and I feel like I can share everything with them.

”

Rosalía, on her sister Pilar Vila Tobella, interview with Lyndsey Havens, *Billboard*, 5 November 2025

“

With *Los Ángeles*, I wanted to establish my musical legacy… and honour the classic sound of flamenco in the most traditional sense, respecting them to the maximum, with a pop and experimental structure, but with very basic instrumentation and a minimalist sound – just guitar and voice.

”

Rosalía, on her debut album *Los Ángeles* (2016) – not the city, but something darker, more spiritual: death, and meeting the angels, interview with Ecleen Luzmila Caraballo, Jezebel, 2 November 2018

“

Flamenco is connected with so many types of music. It has Jewish culture inside, Arabian culture inside, Russian culture inside, Spanish culture inside. It's linked to African music too, because African music has the '*amalgama*' rhythms you can find in flamenco. You can find everything in flamenco. That's why it's so beautiful.

”

Rosalía, on flamenco's global origins, interview with Mark Savage, BBC, 7 January 2019

At 16, Rosalía had surgery on her vocal cords after seriously damaging her voice – the kind of setback that could've ended everything before it even started.

"I couldn't speak for a month – it was very strange, like this fasting of speaking, and then a year of vocal rehabilitation. Afterwards, it took me so many years to really feel like I could actually use my instrument", she told the *The Guardian* in 2025.

When her voice came back, she started training in classical singing – and learnt the right way, the safe way to look after her voice.

CHAPTER TWO

KNOW YOURSELF

"I know exactly who I am." Rosalía says it best herself on the track "Berghain" from LUX.

This chapter dives into her influences, her obsessions, and the things that shape her world – showing us a clearer picture of who she is.

Because if there's one thing that's certain, she already knows.

"The beauty of art is putting things on the table and proposing questions – and probably finding more questions than answers."

Rosalía, on the endless curiosity she finds in making art and the creative process, interview with Laura Snapes, *The Guardian*, 7 November 2025

"

In order to fully enjoy music, you have to have a tolerant, open way of understanding it. Because music is the '4'33"' of [experimental composer] John Cage, as much as the birds in the trees for the Kaluli of New Guinea, as much as the fugues of Bach, as much as the songs of [Puerto Rican singer] Chencho Corleone. All of it is music. And if you understand that, then you can enjoy in a much fuller, profound way, what music is.

"

Rosalía, on her interest in all forms of music, interview with Lyndsey Havens, *Billboard*, 5 November 2025

“What is the quality I like most in men? That he’s gay.”

Rosalía, on men (a joke, right?), interview with Alex Ocho, Complex, 5 March 2026

“

I try to trust my intuition as much as possible. Not knowing or not having an answer to something makes you move forward, makes you keep going towards finding it.

”

Rosalía, on relying on her gut instincts to drive her career and music, Stylecaster, 10 February 2023

> “When rage is pure, it can be *ecstatic*.”

Rosalía, on anger as a positive creative state of mind, *Vogue*, 10 February 2026

"

Los Ángeles was an album with which I wanted to revindicate and rescue popular lyrics and melodies, to be faithful to the material, but experiment with the form on guitar. For *El Mal Querer*, I wanted to experiment with electronic music and develop an idea that I'd had since I was 17. The idea of flamenco and sampling. Because electronic music forms part of my background. I wanted to develop a project that had the voice at the forefront, a lot of harmonies, very rhythmic – and nothing like *Los Ángeles*.

"

Rosalía, on comparing 2018's *El Mal Querer* album with her 2017 debut *Los Ángeles*, *Billboard*, 29 October 2018

“

Anaïs Nin [the famous French writer] once said, ‘We write to taste life twice’. I love that quote so much. I think a good song can let you taste life twice. It can make you re-experience a moment twice. Ten years after you hear a song, it’s going to make you re-live, re-experience that moment again. So, I am very honoured to be a songwriter.

”

Rosalía, on her pride at her life’s vocation, interview with Erica Gonzales, *Elle*, 19 February 2026

Rosalía’s surname, Tobella, traces back to medieval Spain, with likely roots from the name Tobias that means “God is good” in Hebrew.

“

So many times people reduce a woman and her talent by limiting her to a prefabricated category. Pure cliché – the crazy one, the girlboss, the witch, the messy one, the histrionic, the diva. I hope I can dissipate all those useless categories, and take a little bit from each of them, play with all of them in my projects.

”

Rosalía, on her desire to destroy, and have fun with, societal gender clichés, interview with Shaad D’Souza, *The Guardian*, 8 December 2022

28 March 2019

The day Rosalía levelled up – again. This marked the release of her second collaboration with J Balvin, "Con Altura" (meaning "With Height"). Its famous video, directed by Director X, became one of the most-watched of 2019 by a female artist, amassing more than 2.2 billion views to date.

Its sharp, swagger-heavy choreography, including flamenco-inspired *braceo* (arm movements), went viral and the track won two MTV Video Music Awards – Best Latin Video and Best Choreography – making Rosalía one of the first Spanish artists to take home a VMA.

"I'm working harder now than at any other point in my life because I have a fear of losing what I have. Before, I had nothing. And I had nothing to lose. So I've always been fearless."

Rosalía, on her fearless, all-in work ethic, interview with Michael Cragg, *The Guardian*, 28 June 2019

“

To me, everything comes from the voice. When I hear someone talk, when I hear someone communicate, the sound – it gives me a lot of information, more than just what they're saying. There's a lot of magic in voices. I love voices that are very old, very gravelly, very deep. I like metallic voices; I like velvety voices. The voices of children.

”

Rosalía, on her love of the sound a voice makes, interview with Isabelia Herrera, *The FADER*, Summer 2019

"Every day, I try to put on a cute look. I try to choose a fragrance that's going to lift me up if I need that, or it's going to make me feel more sensual if I need that. At the end of the day, I try to live paying attention to details and putting love into details because that's what really keeps me going through the day."

Rosalía, on her intimitable fashion sense and style – and knowing that it's all about the details, interview with Erica Gonzales, *Elle*, 19 February 2026

"

I try to receive the energy and not focus on somebody. I just try to focus on the lyrics, the music, keyboards, percussion, clappers, flamenco singers. There's a lot going on! It's not easy. I'm dancing and singing at the same time, no playback at all – no playback AT ALL!

"

Rosalía, on her commitment to live performances, interview with Stuart Brumfitt, *The Face*, 5 September 2019

“I feel like on *MOTOMAMI* I did and said exactly what I wanted to say and do, on my own terms. After this, there’s no turning back.”

Rosalía, on 2022’s album *MOTOMAMI* being a defining statement, interview with Cat Cardenas, *Rolling Stone*, 13 December 2022

“

If Latin music is music made in Spanish, then my music is part of Latin music. But I do know that if I say I'm a Latina artist, that's not correct, is it? I'm part of a generation that's making music in Spanish. So, I don't know! I'd prefer for others to decide if I'm included in that, no?

”

Rosalía, on whether she's considered a Latin or Hispanic artist, interview with Isabelia Herrera, *The FADER*, Summer 2019

15 November 2018

The night Rosalía took home her first Latin Grammy.

Winning Best Alternative Song and Best Urban Fusion/Performance for "Malamente", she used her moment to shine a light on the female artists who inspired her:

"This is incredible. It's a dream… Thank you so much for all the love, thanks all of you for the recognition, I am proud to lead my project and always make music that represents me, despite the risk, and to be able to share it with the world and be here. I want to thank women like Lauryn Hill, Björk, Kate Bush… shout out to all the women in the industry that have taught me that I could do this because thanks to them I am here."

"

It's very important not to take failure too seriously: failure can turn into success if you know what to do with it! Many times in the studio, a mistake brings with it a new possibility, opens a new path. For me, success is when I feel aligned between what I think, feel, and do: when I know who I am and live according to that as much as possible.

"

Rosalía, on failure and success, interview with Tobias Hess, *Paper*, 7 August 2025

"

There are artists of all kinds. There are artists who are here to remind us where we come from; there are artists who are here to show us where to go, you know? Honestly, I don't know what kind of artist I am! I don't know what my work will mean in a few years. But I am clear that above all else I am experimental. It's a necessity for me. I don't know how to live any other way. I don't know how to do anything else. There is no alternative.

"

Rosalía, on the the kind of artists she sees herself as, interview with Isabelia Herrera, *The FADER*, Summer 2019

Studio Albums

Los Ángeles

Released: 10 February 2017

El Mal Querer

Released: 2 November 2018

MOTOMAMI

Released: 18 March 2022

LUX

Released: 7 November 2025

"

My mom told me, whatever I do in life, go for it full on. I don't remember her words exactly, but I remember how they sounded. She told me that I had to put my all into it.

"

Rosalía, on advice from her mother, interview with Fernando Navarro, *El País*, 12 March 2022

“

Constant online connection creates distraction. I have a box with a timer where I can put my phone inside, and it won’t open until the time runs out. It’s very useful.

”

Rosalía, on limiting screen time to maximize her focus while in the creative zone, interview with Tobias Hess, *Paper*, 7 August 2025

“

I compose, produce, arrange – I don't just perform. I'm playing keyboards, playing bass, doing everything. At the end of the day, I'm the one working my fingers to the bone.

”

Rosalía, on how she takes charge of all areas of the creative process, interview with Philip Sherburne, Pitchfork, 18 September 2018

"I came across a 13th-century novel called *Flamenca* by an anonymous author. I was struck by the coincidence of the title, which has nothing to do with the musical genre, and began to read it. It's the story of a woman who married a man who becomes consumed with jealousy, and he goes crazy and imprisons her. And it got me thinking, almost anthropologically: Centuries later, have we altered the ways in which we love and relate to other people, or are we still acting in the same ways?"

Rosalía, on "toxic love" – the concept behind 2018's *El Mal Querer*, interview with Philip Sherburne, Pitchfork, 18 September 2018

“

I always do something that nobody expects. Because for me, that’s what makes sense. And that’s the point of being a musician.

”

Rosalía, on her desire to be different with each new album and era, interview with Stuart Brumfitt, *The Face*, 5 September 2019

“

I don’t remember one video shoot when I haven’t ended either with some dirt or crazy sparkles and paint all over my body!

”

Rosalía, on her obsession with creating viral music videos – the kind you *feel* as much as you watch, interview with Erica Gonzales, *Elle*, 19 February 2026

“

The women in my life are my main inspiration. *MOTOMAMI* wouldn’t exist without my grandma, my mom, my sister. I have so much love for them and that’s why I’m a motomami, because they were a motomami before me. My mom was the OG motomami. She would have this long blonde curly hair and she would be driving a Harley when I was a kid, and I hugged her while she was driving.

I remember the wind in her hair in front of my helmet in Barcelona. Because of the experiences I've had with my family, nowadays I feel like: 'Oh, I'm a *woman*'.

”

Rosalía, on the incredible women in her life who inspire her, interview with Julianne Escobedo Shepherd, Pitchfork, 18 May 2022

CHAPTER THREE

LIKE A PRAYER

Even though she sings in 14 languages on *LUX*, Rosalía mostly sticks to Spanish – and somehow still connects with people everywhere.

No translation needed. Whether it's raw, sometimes-controversial lyrics or themes like mysticism, feminine power and identity, she always has something to say.

Think of this chapter as her confessional.

"I think that the more we are in the era of dopamine, the more I want the opposite. At least that's what I want. That's what I'm *craving*."

Rosalía, on social media and the fake dopamine hits that come with it, interview with Joe Coscarelli and Jon Caramanica, *The New York Times*, 7 November 2025

“

When I write a song, there are spaces left blank. You pour out, and you don’t have a total sense of what the final result will be. You have to find what’s missing, fill the gaps, and if you leave it there a bit, maybe what’s needed will arrive. I think there’s always a crack. I know my work will be imperfect because it’s human, and I accept that from the start.

”

Rosalía, on her deliberately "imperfect" songwriting process, interview with Xavi Sancho, *El País*, 9 November 2025

“

Whenever I perform, I always try to find that moment when you're not there as an artist, when you're nothing more than a channel for the song's soul to pass through to an audience. You're there more than ever, and super awake, but at the same time you're gone.

”

Rosalía, on her passion for connecting with fans during live performances, interview with Marcela Valdes, *The New York Times*, 8 October 2019

26 January 2020

The night Rosalía made the 62nd Grammy Awards all hers. Performing "Juro Que", she became the first female Spanish artist to take the stage at the ceremony – and she didn't play it safe.

Performing barefoot, raw, and completely free, she owned it. She was celebrating: she was now the first Spanish-language act in Grammy history to be nominated for Best New Artist. The world has belonged to her ever since.

"My voice is my instrument, and the albums are built around my voice, but it's the piano that allows me to write songs. The piano helps, because I am always looking to see where the harmony can coexist with the melody. I get very serious about it when I'm sitting at the piano."

Rosalía, on her second favourite instrument – the piano, interview with Xavi Sancho, *El País*, 9 November 2025

> “If my situation were different, I would be studying, going back to college to study philosophy and theology.”

Rosalía, on what she'd be doing if she wasn't a global superstar, interview with Aureliano Tonet, *Le Monde*, 22 January 2026

“We all want love – brotherly love, divine love, carnal love.”

Rosalía, on love in all its complex forms, interview with Alex Peters, *Dazed*, 3 March 2026

Rosalía's second album, the critically acclaimed *El Mal Querer* (2018), is a fusion of traditional flamenco with urban, experimental pop.

The record began as Rosalía's final degree project at the Catalonia College of Music, where she studied Interpretation of Flamenco and graduated in 2017.

“The artist who walks beside the devil, putting a hand on his shoulder, can expand our understanding of wickedness.”

Rosalía, on her favourite quote (origin unknown), which explains how there has to be darkness in order for the light shine bright, interview with Tom Skinner, *NME*, 11 November 2025

“

She was a hermit, she was supposed to get married. And then she decided not to the day before the wedding. I found that coincidence pretty insane.

”

Rosalía, on the Sicilian saint whose name she bears, Santa Rosalía de Palermo (and perhaps a coded reference to her former fiancé Rauw Alejandro), interview with Aureliano Tonet, *Le Monde*, 22 January 2026

“

I am inspired by irreverent women like Joan of Arc, Aretha Franklin, Nina Simone, Patti Smith, Cher – divas. They carry the weight and they… *endure*. What I love about them is that they are unapologetic about what they want and what they do, what their path is. That's a guide, *un faro* – a lighthouse. Through time, 'diva' has had this negative connotation. But nowadays I don't feel like it has the same way, and I celebrate women that are unapologetic and that do their path.

”

Rosalía, on divas: her songwriting inspiration, interview with Laura Snapes, *The Guardian*, 7 November 2025

“

Red is my favourite colour. It has always been a strong and powerful colour. It’s a very flamenco colour – and flamenco is my main inspiration.

”

Rosalía, on her favourite colour, interview with Thatiana Diaz, Refinery29, 31 August 2020

"Leonard Cohen [Canadian songwriter] used to say everyone has a song. If it's true that every poet has a poem, every filmmaker a film, and every musician a song inside them, then I hope I never find mine."

Rosalía, on her desire to never be truly defined artistically, interview with Abby Aguirre, *Vogue*, 10 February 2026

"Reggaeton doesn't ask for forgiveness or permission. That's why I thought it was a perfect fit for *MOTOMAMI*. In the end, it's very direct and raw music, and people are not used to celebrating women who speak like that."

Rosalía, on reggaeton – the main music genre on *MOTOMAMI*, interview with Fernando Navarro, *El País*, 12 March 2022

"

Loneliness is my lesson in this life. I struggle so much with feeling lonely. I really don't like loneliness. I'm a very social person. I like to be surrounded by my friends. I like to be surrounded by my family.

"

Rosalía, on loneliness, interview with Daniela Avila, *People*, 30 November 2025

"

My career is going to be a love letter to the styles of music I love. In the future I will add whatever genres I come across. In music there is no right and wrong, good or bad. What matters is that the music reflects *me*.

"

Rosalía, on her future path and how it must reflect who she is, interview with Fernando Navarro, *El País*, 12 March 2022

“The pandemic was very hard. I was almost away from my family for two years. I was away from the neighborhood where I grew up. Away from my old friends. Far away from everything. I did it to fully commit to my record. But it was hard. There were moments when I was really alone.”

Rosalía, on the mental health impact of the 2020 coronavirus pandemic and lockdown isolation, interview with Fernando Navarro, *El País*, 12 March 2022

"Transformation, sexuality, heartbreak, celebration, spirituality, self-respect."

Rosalía, on the most essential themes found in her music, interview with Diego Ortiz, *Rolling Stone*, 17 November 2021

“

I love having a significant other and sharing with a significant other. I love affection. I think that I always need to have faith in love.

”

Rosalía, on the importance of love in her life, interview with Daniela Avila, People, 30 November 2025

At 19, Rosalía spent 33 days walking the 500-mile Camino de Santiago pilgrimage across northern Spain – on her own. Partly out of devotion and partly from a place of defiance.

"Somebody in my family said I wouldn't be able to do it because I wasn't prepared physically," she told the *The Guardian* in 2025. "But I learned that if I could do this one thing, I could do other things."

While there, she manifested her goal of becoming a professional musician. "I was like, 'If I can do this camino from the beginning until the end, that's going to be a sign that I can pursue a career in music,'" she told *Vogue* in 2026.

"I love the operatic, the drama, a wig here and there and a little bit of fantasy."

Rosalía, on her passion for dressing up in her music videos, interview with Alex Peters, *Dazed*, 3 March 2026

"

My mother is a very strong, independent leader. My sister is also very inspiring, so my natural surroundings have been very feminine. I make music with many men, but my team is mostly women. It's a little bit about vindication for women, too. As we see more women in positions of power in the industry, it will have an influence. Having more women in power means we're all rowing in the same direction.

"

Rosalía, on her desire to see more women in positions of power, interview with Leila Cobo, *Billboard*, 12 December 2019

“

I didn’t begin my career by making hits. If I have any, it’s thanks to the people who have shown their support. I think I’ll try to continue working like this, working on projects, making music I believe in. If I happen to have a big song, cool! I’ll throw a party, I’ll have an absolute blast, I’ll be thrilled, I’ll celebrate and feel thankful for it.

”

Rosalía, on writing hit songs, interview with Diego Ortiz, *Rolling Stone*, 17 November 2021

“

There are people who think that music can be made by algorithms. One doesn’t make a lyric, distort a voice or choose an asymmetrical structure thinking about numbers. It’s done for the feeling. You look for emotion.

”

Rosalía, on choosing not to write songs based on what might sell, interview with Fernando Navarro, *El País*, 12 March 2022

“

Mysticism has been *the* main inspiration since I began building the universe of *LUX*. Phrases like that of Rabia Al-Adawiyya where she says: ‘No woman ever claimed to be God’; ‘I am not afraid, I was born to do this’ by Joan of Arc, or ‘Be who God meant you to be and you will set the world on fire’ from St Catherine of Siena. They are always in my head and accompany me during my day, while I have breakfast, do my hair or tidy my room.

”

Rosalía, on what inspired her lyrics on 2025’s *LUX*, interview with Alex Peters, *Dazed*, 3 March 2026

"

I've always listened to Lil' Kim, I've always listened to Tupac. It's not that different for me to make a song where I'm rapping. It's using my voice in various ways, because my voice is an instrument – it's absurd to use it in one way only.

"

Rosalía, on her earliest rap influences, interview with Diego Ortiz, *Rolling Stone*, 17 November 2021

"

The other day I read that Mozart had Tourette's. He invented words, he wrote backwards and upside down, he would change language several times – apparently he would write in German and then freely jump to French, Italian or Latin. And that music would come from that freedom. That's how I feel as a musician – it's really hard for me not to create from this place of freedom.

"

Rosalía, on her desire to feel free while making music – and why *LUX* contains her singing in 14 languages, interview with Julianne Escobedo Shepherd, *Pitchfork*, 18 May 2022

"

If success ends up breaking me over the years, well, that's life and that's the journey. Life and death are very close to each other.

"

Rosalía, on the perils of overwhelming global success, interview with Fernando Navarro, *El País*, 12 March 2022

CHAPTER FOUR

HURTS LIKE HEAVEN

Since 2018, Rosalía has been carving out her own path, turning traditional Spanish sounds into something the whole world can't get enough of.

Here, we're celebrating her journey – from music student to full-on global icon.

> “It’s a lot more interesting to dig into the popular music from where I’m from than adhere to some kind of standardized global pop.”

Rosalía, on staying true to her Spanish roots, interview with Judy Cantor-Navas, *Billboard*, 27 August 2018

"

I belong to the world. That's how I feel – *yo no soy tan mía como del mundo.**

"

Rosalía, on her new-found status as a pop phenomenon, *The New York Times*, 7 November 2025

* "I'm not as much mine as I am the world's."

“

The price you pay, the sacrifice, the amount of moments that you lose with your family, with your loved ones. My grandpa died when I was at the Latin Grammys in 2019, and I was about to perform when I found out. I couldn’t even be at the burial. Those things, I’ll have to live with the sadness and the regret of not being there.

Those are things that are not the good side of being a musician: always struggling, always being committed to whatever you're doing, to the people who are there in the audience that night... The price is really high, but this is what I chose.

"

Rosalía, on the price of fame, interview with Lyndsey Havens, *Billboard*, 5 November 2025

"After all the effort and sacrifice I have put into my performances and albums, having people recognize and value my project is very, very meaningful."

Rosalía, on being awarded *Billboard*'s Rising Star award (fellow recipients include Lady Gaga and Ariana Grande), interview with Leila Cobo, Billboard, 12 December 2019

"There's an urge when I make music or go on stage that goes beyond how many people are there. If there was one person in the crowd, I would perform with the exact same energy."

Rosalía, on the energy she conjures for her live performances, interview with Shaad D'Souza, *The Guardian*, 8 December 2022

"As a child, I would always change my Barbies. I'd cut their hair, paint on tattoos, and create new clothes for them. I would invent elaborate stories: fights, dramas, successes. I would try out my ideas on them. And sometimes they would sing! I had big dreams for my Barbies. Even back then with my Barbies, I always knew what I wanted."

Rosalía, on how her Barbie Dolls helped her dream big, interview with Lynn Hirschberg, *W*, 30 September 2019

"

I'm always in constant change. Why, then, shouldn't my sound change with me?

"

Rosalía, on being an ever-evolving artist,
The New York Times, 7 November 2025

“

I don’t make music thinking about money, I don’t make music thinking about awards. I do it because I know this is the reason I’m here.

”

Rosalía, on her simple motivation to make music, interview with Shaad D’Souza, *The Guardian*, 8 December 2022

"

I grew up surrounded by women with long nails. I can't imagine it any other way. Hands have a major presence in flamenco, and when your hands are decorated, it adds power. It's not so much about aesthetics – it's about how I react when my nails are longer and full of colours and texture. It takes me to an expressive place.

"

Rosalía, on her iconic nail game – which is always on point, interview with Leila Cobo, *Billboard*, 12 December 2019

“

I don’t enjoy life only through music – I just enjoy life, period, and I happen to be a musician. But I enjoy life first. It’s amazing!

”

Rosalía, on her desire to live life to its fullest, interview with Julianne Escobedo Shepherd, Pitchfork, 18 May 2022

“

My sister says that my music is not pop. But I want to think that my music is pop. It's just another way of making pop. There has to exist another way of making it pop! Björk proved it. Kate Bush proved it. And I need to think that what I'm doing is pop, because otherwise I don't think that I am succeeding. What I want to do is make music that hopefully a lot of people can enjoy.

”

Rosalía, on defining her (pop?) sound, interview with Joe Coscarelli and Jon Caramanica, *The New York Times*, 7 November 2025

“

I never had a Plan B. I always had the intuition and the faith that singing would be my life and that it couldn’t be any other way, no matter the level. I have big dreams, but if God would’ve told me that I had to sing in a local bar in Barcelona, and that that would be my life, that would be my life. I would’ve done it with the same passion. Singing is the most pure form I know of communicating.

”

Rosalía, on singing as her *sole* vocation, interview with Ecleen Luzmila Caraballo, Jezebel, 2 November 2018

The title of Rosalía's Grammy-winning 2022 album, *MOTOMAMI*, is a collision of energies – masculine and feminine, hard and soft, all at once.

"Moto" represents power, speed and strength; "Mami" signifies vulnerability, intimacy and affection.

That tension runs through the entire album, and nowhere is it clearer than on the unforgettable cover, which shows Rosalía naked – except for a motorcycle helmet. Iconic.

Working with Pharrell Williams was a dream. We were in a studio in Los Angeles a few months ago, working on songs. He told me he'd seen 'Aunque es de Noche' and really liked it and wanted to make music with me. I was shocked. It's what I have always wanted to do: work with artists beyond flamenco. Collaborations like that are where you come up with sounds that maybe you wouldn't have found otherwise.

Rosalía, on fulfilling her dream of working with Pharell, interview with Philip Sherburne, Pitchfork, 18 September 2018

“

I really enjoy wearing things that might not be consider considered traditionally ‘pretty’ – like grills or a unibrow. I feel very strong. I think there’s a correlation between strength and beauty. Also, as a musician I love experimenting and that drive I have for discovering new things is often translated to how I choose to look. If I can express who I am through what I wear, I’ll do it!

”

Rosalía, on her unique style, interview with Emily Algar, *Grazia*, 9 June 2021

“

I was so happy that I could sing in Spanish. As a musician, language is almost like another instrument. Every word has a sound. And if this is the first time I’m on television in America, I wanted the world to hear *me*.

”

Rosalía, on performing "Yo x Ti, Tu x Mi" with Ozuna at the 2019 MTV Video Music Awards – opening a cappella, interview with Lynn Hirschberg, *W*, 30 September 2019

"I think that my favourite artists are the ones who don't give you what you want, but what you need."

Rosalía, on her favourite artists and why she likes them, interview with Joe Coscarelli and Jon Caramanica, *The New York Times*, 7 November 2025

"There are two ways to have confidence in oneself. The first is based on the belief that what you do will be successful. The other, by not being afraid of failure. Until now I've always made albums believing they would work."

Rosalía, on her take on confidence, interview with Mar Vallverdú, *Radio Noia*, 16 October 2025

“

I’ve always been passionate about design and sports, and since childhood I’ve always been active – a whirlwind basically. As an adult, it’s the same, so I’m super excited. In fact, if I had a superpower growing up, it was running, running really fast. I loved racing the boys in my class and beating them! Today, I still try to find any excuse to run.

”

Rosalía, on how she always has bags of energy, interview with Rosa Sanchez, *Harper’s Bazaar*, 9 July 2025

"The driving force that leads you to continue making music has to come from a place of purity. Motives like money, pleasure, power... Nothing will come out of there that I'm really interested in. Those are subjects that don't inspire me."

Rosalía, on what motivates her – and what doesn't, interview with Suzy Exposito, *Elle*, 14 August 2025

> *MOTOMAMI* is the most personal story I've told. In my head, *MOTOMAMI* makes sense as a concept, as a feminine figure building herself. It's a self-portrait… a self-portrait in the context of the modern world.

Rosalía, on the concept behind her 2022 album, interview with Diego Ortiz, *Rolling Stone*, 17 November 2021

Rosalía's beloved grandmother – known as Grandma Rosalía – is more than just the singer's namesake.

She's her idol; "she really taught me so much."

Rosalía's dream is to one day have a "big, beautiful family" just like her grandma did.

"I'm excited for that moment in my life one day," she told Pitchfork in 2022.

"

When I was a kid, my grandma would have a lot of Pavarotti records in her place. And she would always be singing while she was washing dishes or whatever. It's funny because it stuck with me. She would say, 'How could you study flamenco?' The real deal, for her, was classical music and classical trained voices. I was like, one day I'm going to make a song that my grandma is going to be like, 'Okay, now you got it.'

"

Rosalía, on why she became a classically trained singer – which she fully showcased on 2025's *LUX*, interview with Anamaria Artemisa Sayre, NPR, 3 November 2025

"I felt less alone being in the studio with her. She's an artist with such a strong drive, who knows exactly who she is and what she wants, who pours her soul out when she sings… no one has impressed me [the way] she has. She has extreme charisma and extreme passion when she sings."

Rosalía, on her 2021 collaboration with Billie Eilish – "Lo Vas a Olvidar", interview with Nuria Net, *Rolling Stone*, 1 June 2019

(Eilish also spoke highly of Rosalía to *Billboard* in 2019: "She actually knows what she wants. That was refreshing because I was like, 'Wow, you're the only other person I've really met that's like this.'")

"

I always feel excited that I can make music in Spanish, and that I can connect with people globally at the same time.

"

Rosalía, on having global crossover appeal without having to compromise or sell-out her language or principles, interview with Thatiana Diaz, Refinery29, 31 August 2020

“

I think of any music genre as a snow globe – you don’t admire it for its stillness. You have to shake it up and see how it explodes.

”

Rosalía, on her genre-bending musical styles, interview with Suzy Exposito, *Rolling Stone*, 20 November 2018

“

I’m rebellious, okay? Let’s say that, for sure, I’m rebellious.

”

Rosalía, on taking pride on being a rebel *with* a cause, interview with Joe Coscarelli and Jon Caramanica, *The New York Times*, 7 November 2025

CHAPTER
FIVE

BACK TO THE FUTURE

At her core, Rosalía is driven by an urge to blend old traditions with a bold, ever-evolving sense of the future.

She moves between opposites – faith and freedom, sex and violence, darkness and light – constantly shifting and reshaping herself.

In a way, she feels like someone meant to bring different worlds together.

“

Being a performer is about being able to be a channel, a vessel. It’s the most fulfilling when you can stop being yourself.

”

Rosalía, on why she loves performing live, interview with Laura Snapes, *The Guardian*, 7 November 2025

“A disorder *and* a superpower.”

Rosalía, when asked, “What does love feel like for you?”, interview with Willa Bennett, High Snobiety, September 2024

“There’s this kind of pressure to be creative or busy most of the time, with lots of activities and progress, and I’m trying to run from that. I’m trying to do things that help keep me mentally healthy, and if that includes making music, then great. But I won’t lie – there are days when I just watch a show and eat a packet of cookies.”

Rosalía, on the pressure to progress, interview with Carina Chocano, *Elle*, 19 May 2020

“

The Grammys experience, really, was like, *Wow*. It was a big deal for me. My whole life, I've watched the artists I most admire perform on that stage. And suddenly, to find myself singing flamenco and dancing a little *seguidilla* [a Spanish dance], I felt so grateful. I felt so embraced. I cried in the car on my way to every rehearsal. I couldn't believe what was happening.

”

Rosalía, on the importance of her first performance at the Latin Grammys, interview with Carina Chocano, *Elle*, 19 May 2020

“

Because of my job, I have to be naked so many times in front of people that I don’t know… I think I’ve kind of developed this detachment with the situation of being naked. And I’ve decided that I don’t care if somebody is seeing me naked, and how they feel about how my body looks, and if they want to look or not… if they want to judge it or not. This is who I am. This is how God made me.

”

Rosalía, on body confidence, interview with James Cabooter, *Daily Star*, 15 November 2025

"

For years, I've been so passionate about nail art and about doing my nails constantly, with different nail artists from around the world. Every time I travel, I want to see how people do it in other places. It's such an ephemeral art, but it's an art – little works of art in miniature.

"

Rosalía, on why her nails are a massive part of her look, interview with Carina Chocano, *Elle*, 19 May 2020

“

I’m glad that my struggle to survive on an American film set ended up translating into me being funny on camera, because girl… that wasn’t easy! My *first job* acting on a series and it’s *Euphoria*? In music, I’m the director, I call the shots, I’m on everything from the biggest thing to the smallest. I build my own structure, rhythm and scenario. In *Euphoria*, it’s the opposite and was scary in a very, very different way.

”

Rosalía, on her appearance as Magick, a stripper working at the Silver Slipper nightclub on *Euphoria*, season three, interview with Alex Peters, *Dazed*, 3 March 2026

“

The first video I ever made on my YouTube channel – you can still see it – is of me singing the only cover I've ever done. It was Frank Ocean's 'Thinkin Bout You'. Oh my God!

”

Rosalía, on her first ever YouTube upload, interview with Carina Chocano, *Elle*, 19 May 2020

(The video's hashtag #normcore references a fashion 'anti-trend' of the 2010s: unpretentious, mundane, 'normal' clothing. In the video, Rosalía wears a simple red hoodie and a black T-shirt. Rare!)

"Life, love, fighting, spirituality, death – you can find everything in flamenco. That's why I love the music so much."

Rosalía, on the lyrical themes of flamenco – and how they resonate, interview with Bradley Stern, *Paper*, 2 November 2018

15 April 2023

The night Rosalía turned Coachella into Motochella. Taking over the main stage, her set quickly became the biggest, most packed of the weekend.

Dressed in a customised Harley-Davidson black-and-white helmet, black leather trousers and a pink robe, she brought full *MOTOMAMI* energy to the Californian desert.

Addressing her "motobabies", she said: "*Buenas noches*, Coachella! I feel very happy to see you all here today. You fill my heart with your presence. I come from Barcelona, that's why this stage is so special. It's because of you that I'm here."

Rosalía's fandom may go by several names – motomamis, motopapis, motobabies, Ángeles, and even Rosalíans – but her fans have only one name for their favourite artist: "Diosalía", a blend of her name and the Spanish word for "God".

“

My goal is to bridge the beauty of the past and history with the present. I want to be traditional, and yet not old.

”

Rosalía, on her mission to unite her heritage with new ideas, interview with Lynn Hirschberg, *W*, 30 September 2019

"There are times when your music will connect with people. There are times when not so much. Times when you'll feel really, really connected; times when not so much. But that's a part of this kind of work and you need to accept it. At the same time, that humility makes it difficult to fail and keeps you connected to why you create in the first place."

Rosalía, on understanding that her music will not always be *en vogue*, interview with Ecleen Luzmila Caraballo, Jezebel, 2 November 2018

"

Nowadays, more than ever, I feel like it's necessary to understand the other. In a world that sometimes feels so divided, for me it's about collecting stories and making songs out of that the best I can, because it's the love for the other that allows me to do an album like *LUX*.

"

Rosalía, on the importance of trying to understand other people, interview with Laura Snapes, *The Guardian*, 7 November 2025

"

I see a lot of this cancel culture happening for everyone. That is always strange to me. I think there's a need of much more culture of forgiveness. I wouldn't cancel a friend because we think different. And definitely, I always feel like I have so much to learn and I always try to do things better. But at the same time, I like a lot something that Roland Barthes [a French philosopher] said about the 'anti-hero… who can bear contradiction without shame'.

We all have contradictions. It's impossible not to in a world as imperfect and contradictory as the one we live in. So I try to stay connected with what my mission is, which is to make music from the most loving place possible.

”

Rosalía, on being misunderstood and cancel culture, interview with Laura Snapes, *The Guardian*, 7 November 2025

"The love I feel and my connection to the spiritual… the best way I have to express it is by making songs. *LUX* is an album about love, inspired by the lives of these saints, by feminine mysticism. They are saints from all over the world, from different cultures and religions, and all of this has allowed me to learn, which was ultimately the thing I was most excited about: expanding my horizons and my idea of spirituality. I also think this is an album about the other, about understanding the other."

Rosalía, on expanding her spiritual horizons, interview with Xavi Sancho, *El País*, 9 November 2025

"The divas who inspire me are irreverent and strong, they know what they want and they don't apologize for it. I never see myself like that, but I'm not upset if other people perceive me like that!"

Rosalía, on her "diva" persona, interview with Aureliano Tonet, *Le Monde*, 22 January 2026

"I just want to have fun making music – and the only way is always trying to do it different. You want extremes. You want oppositites. It's like a pendulum. In *MOTOMAMI* it was about inventing words. On *LUX*, it's like, let me try to figure out a way to make lyrics that can be set in stone."

Rosalía, on the differences between her albums, interview with Nick Grimshaw, BBC 6 Music, 7 November 2025

"I love travelling, I love learning from other humans. Why would I not try to learn another language and try to sing in another language and expand the way I can be a singer or a musician or an artist? The world is so connected."

Rosalía, on learning to sing in 14 languages on *LUX* and pushing her voice to its limits, interview with Joe Coscarelli and Jon Caramanica, *The New York Times*, 7 November 2025

“All the albums I’ve done helped me be able to be the musician I am today and make this album now. *LUX* wouldn’t exist if I hadn’t taken the previous steps. Each album helped me release something, to free myself as much as possible. Every time I go to the studio, it’s from wanting to play around, try something different, to find different styles of making songs. I always try to stay open.”

Rosalía, on how her past musical experiences help evolve her future, interview with Lyndsey Havens, *Billboard*, 5 November 2025

"

I feel like a kid on a playground. Since *El Mal Querer* I've been able to go to the studio with some artists that I admire and just have fun.

"

Rosalía, on enjoying her time in the studio, interview with Diego Ortiz, *Rolling Stone*, 17 November 2021

"What is all this crazy life for? I think it is to crack a few jokes and have random experiences with incredible minds that expand your own."

Rosalía, on life and its meaning, interview with Alex Peters, *Dazed*, 3 March 2026

“

I didn’t think twice about whether to go on tour with *LUX* or not. Even though the tour life is so hard and you can so easily become mentally unstable, I think it’s worth it for two main reasons: to share with my fans and to try to get lucky and find truth on stage.

”

Rosalía, on why she’s taking *LUX* on a 57-date world tour throughout 2025–26 to more than one million fans (despite not liking tour life!), interview with Alex Peters, *Dazed*, 3 March 2026

“

Performing is an act for others. I don’t like touring. I like to be onstage and I love my fans, so I do it. But I love being in my home, calm, reading, cooking, going to the gym, lifting weights and going to sleep. Literally, that makes me so happy; I don’t need a lot.

”

Rosalía, on tour life versus home life, interview with Lyndsey Havens, *Billboard*, 5 November 2025

In March 2019, Rosalía made her film debut in Pedro Almodóvar's *Dolor y Gloria* (*Pain and Glory*), appearing alongside Penélope Cruz and Antonio Banderas. The film follows an ageing Spanish director reflecting on his life and work at a creative crossroads.

In one of its most memorable moments, Rosalía appears with Penélope Cruz in a flashback, singing the Andalusian folk song "A Tu Vera".

In 2023, Cruz told Vogue Spain, "When they told me, 'You have to sing with Rosalía', I thought, 'These people have gone crazy! How am I going to sing with Rosalía?!'"

Rosalía is the first female artist ever to win the Latin Grammy Award for Album of the Year twice – first for *El Mal Querer* in 2019, and again for her bold, experimental 2022 album *MOTOMAMI*.

She is the bookies' favourite to win again for *LUX* in 2027.

"

I think there's too much taboo with certain subjects, and that taboos restrict your freedom. Feminine energy – there's an erotic superiority in femininity. Why not write from there? Why not make a song from that place, where you're owning your desires?

"

Rosalía, on the song "Hentai", and its controversial, explicit lyrics, interview with Shaad D'Souza, *The Guardian*, 8 December 2022

CHAPTER
SIX

SEE THE LIGHT

In 2025, Rosalía dropped her masterpiece *LUX* – Latin for "light". It catapulted her to a whole new level of fame and set her on a path only she can shape from here.

It's an album that feels big, bold and impossible to ignore – and definitely deserves its own chapter. Rosalía, it's time to let your light shine.

"I'm tiring of seeing people referencing celebrities, and celebrities referencing other celebrities. I'm really much more excited about saints."

Rosalía, on the emptiness of fame and the power of saints, interview with Laura Snapes, *The Guardian*, 7 November 2025

“

In general, just to be in this world is a lot; sometimes it’s overwhelming. In the best-case scenario, the idea would be that whoever hears *LUX* feels light and feels hope. Because that was how it was made and where it was made from.

”

Rosalía, on her hope that *LUX* brings some light to its listeners, interview with Lyndsey Havens, *Billboard*, 5 November 2025

"The stories of saints are exceptional. They are remarkable stories about women who lived their lives in a very unconventional way, of women who were writers in very special ways. And so I'm like, 'Let's throw some light there.'"

Rosalía, on her desire to spotlight different female saints' stories on *LUX*, interview with Lyndsey Havens, *Billboard*, 5 November 2025

“

It’s so interesting how much the air is important. At the end of the day, the breath, that’s where it all starts. That’s why in the beginning of *LUX*, after that piano intro, the beginning is a breath. That’s the first human sound on the album.

”

Rosalía, on the importance of the breath, interview with Anamaria Artemisa Sayre, NPR, 3 November 2025

"

LUX has a completely different sound than any of the projects that I've done before. It was a challenge for me to do a more orchestral project and learn how to use an orchestra, understand all the instruments, all the possibilities, and learn and study from amazing composers in history and say, 'Okay, that's what's been done. And what can I do that feels personal and honest for me?'

"

Rosalía, on the grand, classical orchestrata on *LUX*, interview with Lyndsey Havens, *Billboard*, 5 November 2025

“

I was recording *LUX* while I was shooting *Euphoria*. I had to divide my mind between both and it was also the first time that I was doing something like this – preparing a character, studying lines. These are new things for me and I'm not used to it. It's very different from making an album and making music. For some reason, I didn't completely go crazy, and we're still here.

”

Rosalía, on her TV acting debut on *Euphoria* (2026) as an escape from creating *LUX*, interview with Lyndsey Havens, *Billboard*, 5 November 2025

Rosalía's 2025 magnum opus *LUX* did more than just see the light – it bedazzled the whole world. Clocking over 42 million Spotify streams in a single day, it became the biggest one-day debut for a Spanish-speaking female artist in history.

The success didn't stop there: *LUX* hit No. 1 across five *Billboard* album charts at once – Latin, Latin Pop, Classical, Classical Crossover, and World.

Total global domination.

“

Nobody forces me to do anything. I decide that my mission in life is to make music. I am at the service of the mission of making music.

”

Rosalía, on being her own boss – and being on a mission from God, interview with Xavier Cervantes, *ARA*, 16 October 2025

“

Santa Olga de Kyiv, who lived in the 10th century, converted to Christianity and was considered a saint because she brought so many people to that religion. But she was an assassin – when her husband was killed, she, out of revenge, killed a lot of men. It’s crazy that person can become a saint. In different religions, contexts, cultures, sainthood is understood so differently.

”

Rosalía, on her fresh take on sainthood, interview with Laura Snapes, *The Guardian*, 7 November 2025

"

The more free my body is, the better my voice sounds. I used to sing in *Tablaos*, these traditional places where they played flamenco music and I used to watch how the dancers moved. I have always been attentive to all the detail.

"

Rosalía, on the origins of her viral dance moves, interview with Mark Savage, BBC, 7 January 2019

“

I can tell you a year of making *LUX* was spent only on the lyrics: reading and writing lyrics. Another year only for arrangements, production, recording. That year of reading and writing lyrics was a period of isolation, of staying at home and doing nothing else. Basically, simplifying my days to the maximum. I can’t write sitting up, only lying down. Lying down, head supported, laptop on my lap… like that all day.

Personally, I'd prefer to be able to write lyrics while going to the studio, hanging out with my friends... Because that would be a more enjoyable process, but in that way I wouldn't be able to produce this. Over the years, I've understood how my process works.

Rosalía, on her unique creative process, interview with Xavi Sancho, *El País*, 9 November 2025

"Throughout *LUX*, I am looking for the sweet spot, that balance or blurred line between the personal and the universal."

Rosalía, on connecting with people through her music, interview with Xavi Sancho, *El País*, 9 November 2025

"

I'd never want to put out records with a sense of urgency, or with the pressure of, 'Oh, it's been X years.' I don't think I'm going to be that type of artist. I think I'm always going to make music when I feel like I have something to say.

"

Rosalía, on not rushing to release music, interview with Cat Cardenas, *Rolling Stone*, 13 December 2022

“

I understand that a lot of people can’t connect with my music, because it’s a radical proposal and a personal proposal. I understand the risk I take in making these decisions with my music.

”

Rosalía, on the daring and often difficult themes in her music, interview with Isabelia Herrera, *The FADER*, Summer 2019

“

As an artist, my biggest desire is to be as free as possible. How far can I push to get as much freedom as possible in many ways, in subjects, in sound, in aesthetic, in everything?

”

Rosalía, on her desire to find ultimate freedom as an artist, interview with Cat Cardenas, *Rolling Stone*, 13 December 2022

“

I was trying to find an image that would symbolize feminine spirituality. To me this was the one that could translate how this album sounds, what this album is about, where I'm singing from, and the inspiration behind it.

”

Rosalía, on the iconic *LUX* cover artwork (where she's dressed in a nun-insired habit), interview with Abby Aguirre, *Vogue*, 10 February 2026

To date, Rosalía has racked up more than 15 billion streams on Spotify.

Her biggest hitters so far?

"Despechá" (from *MOTOMAMI*) and "La Noche De Anoche" with Puerto Rican powerhouse – and the world's hottest male artist – Bad Bunny; both pulling in more than 1.5 billion streams each.

“

So many saints were nuns. I found it so amazing to learn about their lives, learn about how they would express themselves. They would have an experience of God, and they would explain it with words. It was another way of understanding *lo divino*.

”

Rosalía, on the cultural and religious signifance of nuns, interview with Abby Aguirre, *Vogue*, 10 February 2026

“The audience is essential in my performances, they complete them. My music feels different when I share it with others. I feel a strong energy coming towards me when I’m on stage; I try my best to give the energy back and be generous in the way I perform.”

Rosalía, on interacting with the audience at her live shows, interview with Lea Veloso, StyleCaster, 10 February 2023

“There’s only a risk if there’s something to lose.”

Rosalía, on being a go-getter, interview with Fernando Navarro, *El País*, 12 March 2022

"Just the other day, I was wondering what genre do we put *LUX* under when it goes to stores, and, honestly, I don't know. It draws from music all over the world – from classical music, from flamenco. It has pop ambition but also experimental elements, because the whole process was experimental. I have no idea. I'll let others decide where it belongs when they hear it."

Rosalía, on *LUX* being genre-bending and unclassifiable, interview with Marcos Hassan, Remezcla, 7 November 2025

“I have the luck to be able to collaborate with great people like Antón Álvarez, Pablo Díaz-Reixa [AKA El Guincho] who co-produced *El Mal Querer*. But I’m responsible for my work and my sound. It’s important to me that people know that women can lead their own projects.”

Rosalía, on making sure she receives the credit for her work, interview with Ecleen Luzmila Caraballo, Jezebel, 2 November 2018

Rosalía won the inaugural Producer of the Year award at the 2023 *Billboard* Women in Music event, a rare achievement that recognized her crucial hands-on involvement in the arrangement, technical sound design, and production of her highly complex albums, particularly *MOTOMAMI* and, later, *LUX*.

“There are four movements on the album. The first one is about departure, leaving, exiting the pureness. The second one deals with gravity and being a friend of the world, of mundane things. The third one is about grace, being God’s friend. And the fourth one is about goodbyes, about returning home. From that point, I can create a more complete album and I can better explain the light.”

Rosalía, on the four distinct chapters of LUX, interview with Xavi Sancho, *El País*, 9 November 2025

“

I wanted to make an album like *LUX* to push my voice to the limits. I've been preparing for this all my life. While I was making the record, I was remembering how, at the age of 18, I was with my singing teacher and she would teach me opera singing and '*O mio babbino caro*'. I need to make this journey as a songwriter to be able to express myself as a singer.

”

Rosalía, on experimenting with her voice on *LUX*, interview with Xavi Sancho, *El País*, 9 November 2025

“I remember putting up a world map in my room and marking it with pins, trying to understand where each saint was from, what language she spoke, what her story was, and what moved me about it. Then I’d write a song inspired by that. I wanted to find women whose stories were interconnected – unconventional lives, incredible women who were writers, nuns and poets, who found ways to live differently from what was expected of women in their time. Often, becoming a nun gave them the freedom to pursue education and creative work that otherwise wouldn’t have been possible.”

Rosalía, on the lyrical inspiration for *LUX*, interview with Marcos Hassan, Remezcla, 7 November 2025

"I hope with all of my heart that the new generation of women open a path up so that things are different. I'll always render that figure of a strong woman before anything."

Rosalía, on being a strong inspiration for a new generation of Spanish female artists, interview with Julyssa Lopez, *Vogue*, 15 December 2020

“

You’d walk down the hall, and in one classroom there was someone playing flamenco guitar; in the next one someone was studying harp; in the next, someone else was learning a piece by Isaac Albéniz or Chopin on piano. All of it became influences.

”

Rosalía, on her time spent studying at college and its inspiration for her musical eclecticism, interview with Julyssa Lopez, *Vogue*, 15 December 2020

7 November 2025

The day *LUX* lit up the world. Dropping with 42.1 million Spotify streams in its first 24 hours, Rosalía landed the biggest debut of her career and became the first Spanish-speaking solo woman to hit No. 1 on the World Albums chart.

Named after the Latin word for light, *LUX* is a full concept: 18 tracks, each dedicated to a different saint. It draws on the Tower of Babel story from the Book of Genesis, which tells of humanity once speaking a single language before God scattered it into many. That's why Rosalía traverses 14 languages on the album: Spanish, Catalan, English, French, German, Portuguese, Japanese, Hebrew, Arabic, Ukrainian, Mandarin, Latin, Sicilian and Italian.

“

I don’t make music just for myself. I don’t make music just to be happy, I don’t make music just because it completes me. I don’t make music just because I know that I was born to learn how to write songs. It’s for everyone else, it’s for sharing. It would be too selfish of me to make music that only satisfies me. It has to resonate, and sometimes it’s not easy.

”

Rosalía, on why she makes music, interview with Diego Ortiz, *Rolling Stone*, 17 November 2021

"God has blessed me so much in my life, and what better way to give back than by making a record?"

Rosalía, on using her God-given talent, interview with Marcos Hassan, Remezcla, 7 November 2025

“Nowadays, there’s so much division. As a person, I crave the exact opposite. My love is infinite and plural.”

Rosalía, on her life’s driving force, interview with Aureliano Tonet, *Le Monde*, 22 January 2026